Slow and steady
beneath the city
sandy, silty,
grimy, gritty.
Her cutterhead grinds
motor whines
shields keep clear
the churning gears
as she forges a path
shows what can be done
when so many parts
work together as one.

BIG BERTHA

HOW A MASSIVE TUNNEL BORING MACHINE DUG A HIGHWAY UNDER SEATTLE

Amanda Abler

Illustrated by **Katy Wu**

little bigfoot
an imprint of sasquatch books
seattle, wa

On February 28, 2001, the Space Needle began to sway back and forth amid the passing clouds.

Inside, visitors could hear a low rumble climbing up from below. They grasped railings and steadied themselves against walls. All around them, the structure shook like a giant baby rattle. An earthquake was rocking the city of Seattle, Washington.

When the shaking finally stopped, the Alaskan Way Viaduct, an elevated highway that ran along Seattle's waterfront, was badly damaged. The viaduct needed many repairs before it was safe enough for cars to drive on again.

Scientists and Seattleites worried. They knew Seattle was at risk for more earthquakes. What would happen if an even bigger quake hit? The whole roadway might even collapse. Something had to be done.

While city officials argued about what to do, engineers regularly inspected the viaduct for new cracks, ensuring it was still safe enough for traffic.

Then, finally, after eight years and many different ideas, officials announced their plan to tear down the viaduct and dig a tunnel under the city to replace the highway.

When Greg Hauser, a civil engineer living in Seattle, heard about the plan, he knew he wanted to work on the project. His long career in tunnel construction made him the perfect person for the job.

Even as a kid, he had loved
digging holes in his backyard
and turning them into forts.

Greg was delighted when he was hired as the deputy
project manager for the tunnel's construction.

The tunnel under Seattle would need to be enormous—so big that it could hold a double-decker highway! No machine existed that was strong enough and smart enough to dig such a complicated tunnel.

A special tunnel boring machine the height of a five-story building was designed and built in Japan specifically to do the job.

The city of Seattle held a contest to name the machine. A fifth-grade class and a second grader from different schools came up with the same winning name, Bertha, after Bertha Knight Landes, Seattle's first female mayor.

At the time, Bertha was the biggest tunnel boring machine ever built.

In April 2013, Greg greeted Bertha as she arrived in the port of Seattle on a Jumbo ship. Sturdy cranes carefully unloaded her, piece by piece, onto the dock.

A Seattle fireboat, out for its weekly test run, sprayed arches of water high in the air, like open arms welcoming Bertha to Seattle.

Greg thought it was a proper reception for such a magnificent machine.

BIG BERTHA

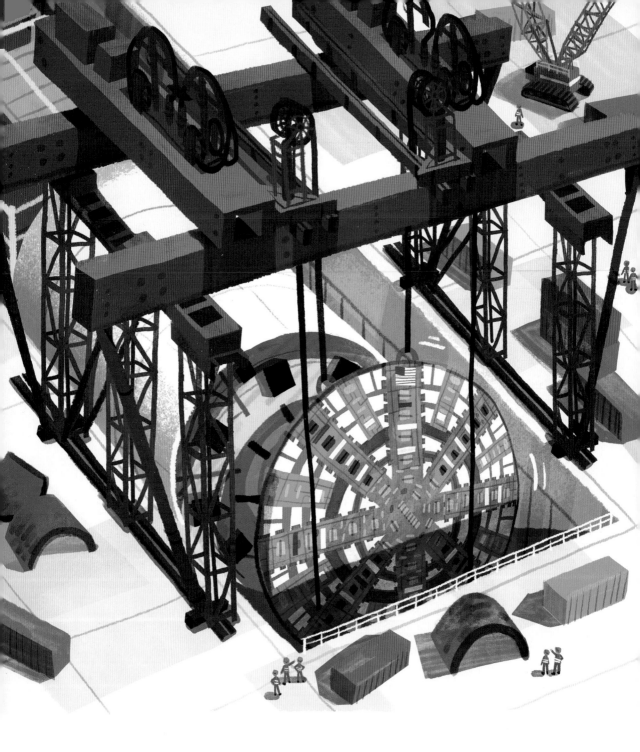

When the launch shaft, the hole where Bertha would begin to dig, was ready, another crane lowered her into the shaft while crews snapped and clicked her pieces together as if she were a giant toy construction set.

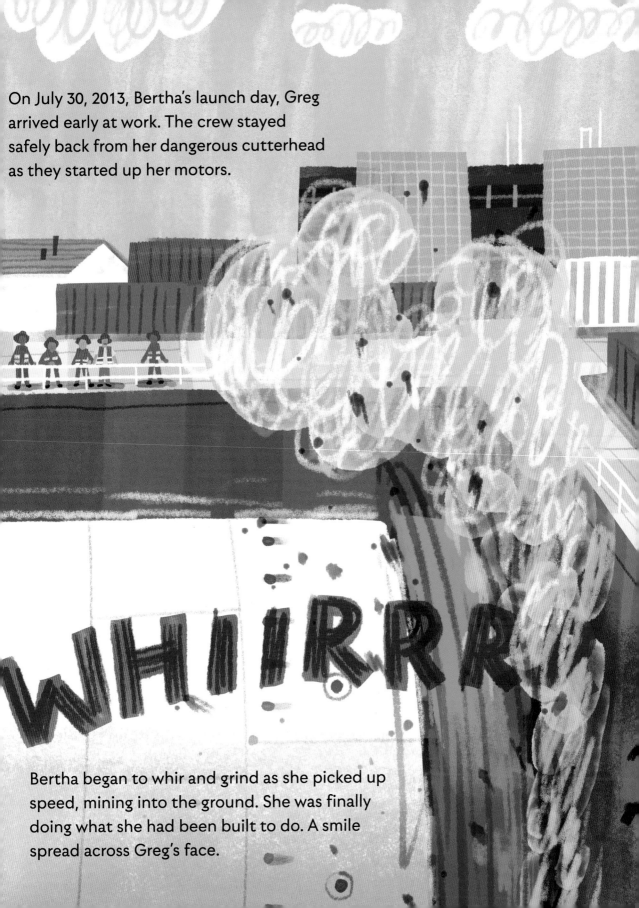

On July 30, 2013, Bertha's launch day, Greg arrived early at work. The crew stayed safely back from her dangerous cutterhead as they started up her motors.

WHIRRR

Bertha began to whir and grind as she picked up speed, mining into the ground. She was finally doing what she had been built to do. A smile spread across Greg's face.

For about four months, Bertha burrowed under the city. Her powerful teeth chewed up dirt and boulders, removing the earth ahead of her.

Meanwhile, her red erector arms pieced together arcs of concrete to form the outer walls of the round tunnel.

As soon as enough tunnel was in place, civil workers began to build the upper level roadway as well. The lower roadway would be added later.

Greg marveled at Bertha's ability to both dig and build the tunnel at the same time while also allowing a separate crew to begin the roadway construction. All this coordination would save a lot of time. Without Bertha, each of these steps would have been completed separately, making the whole process much longer.

As Bertha dug, the sounds of her grinding and screeching on underground rocks was so loud, the crew had to wear earplugs. However, there was no escaping the smell of hot metal and oil from her motors.

Then, in early December 2013, just a few hundred feet from the viaduct, Bertha began to have trouble. As she burrowed through the earth, her motors started to overheat. Had the harsh and challenging ground under Seattle become too much for Bertha? Greg had no choice but to shut her down and find out what was wrong.

Giving Bertha a checkup was a challenge. How was Greg ever going to rescue a giant tunnel boring machine stuck in the ground under the city? He was thankful that at least Bertha's troubles had started before she had dug under the highway. Repairing Bertha while under the viaduct would have been almost impossible.

Because it would be difficult to remove the soil from directly around Bertha, Greg and the team decided to dig a rescue shaft straight down, several feet out in front of her.

Once the shaft was complete, Bertha could grind her way forward, breaking into the open air of the pit. Digging this large hole without the help of Bertha was a slow and difficult task. A whole year passed from the time Bertha broke down until the rescue shaft was finished.

Finally, Greg was ready to get Bertha out of the ground. In mid-February, 2015, the crew started Bertha's motors on low power. Slowly, she ground forward through the earth. Dust filled the air as she inched through the shaft's concrete wall.

Then, crash! Concrete collapsed into the shaft as groundwater that had been under high pressure in front of her gushed out of the hole. The rush of water and earth made a mess, even toppling a porta-potty, but Bertha was free!

A crane lifted Bertha's cutterhead out of the rescue shaft.
She was in worse shape than Greg had feared.

Her cutterhead was torn up, and the outside seals that
protected her motors from dirt and water were broken. Greg
knew Bertha would need much loving care, perhaps even a
complete overhaul, before she was ready to return to her job.

Many Seattleites began to doubt Bertha. Maybe digging this tunnel was too difficult a job. But Greg never lost faith in her.

The months ticked by as the crew fixed her cutterhead and installed new seals, making her stronger than ever. At last, she was ready to get back to work.

In late December, 2015, the crews began test runs on Bertha. Five months later she resumed full digging operations. Greg breathed a sigh of relief.

Now the riskiest part of Bertha's journey was upon her. She needed to dig under the fragile viaduct without accidentally disturbing the ground overhead. If she weren't careful, the viaduct above her could collapse. The less time Bertha spent under it, the less time everyone would be worried about what might happen to the roadway above.

While Bertha tunneled carefully under the viaduct, the crew took turns working and sleeping. But there was no rest for Bertha. Day and night she dug and pieced together the concrete segments of the tunnel behind her, digging and building, digging and building. Then, after two weeks, phew! Bertha had dug all the way under the viaduct.

With the most stressful part of the tunnel behind her, now Bertha could take her time, working during the day and resting at night. Foot by foot, she continued to mine under building after building in downtown Seattle. She even dug right under the Monorail.

On some days, city officials placed balloons on the street to mark the spot where Bertha dug below. People followed the balloons online to see her progress.

As Bertha inched closer to the end of her journey, the crew set up a video camera so Seattleites could watch as Bertha broke through to the outside. This was the moment everyone had been waiting for.

On April 4, 2017, almost four years after Bertha had started her mission, the exit shaft ahead of her began to fill with dust from her grinding. Greg and many others watched as Bertha slowly nosed through the earth one last time. Finally, just before noon and right on time, she broke through. Everyone cheered. Bertha had made it!

Some of the crew blinked back tears. They had grown to love Bertha, and they knew their time together was coming to an end. She would be missed.

After Bertha put the final pieces of the tunnel in place, Greg said goodbye to her. That was the last time he ever saw Bertha. He couldn't bear to go back and see her being taken apart.

Soon, a crane would lift her out of the hole one last time. Her tired and worn parts would be recycled.

However, Greg liked to remember her as he had known her for the past few years, churning and digging in the earth, powerful and reliable, Seattle's big Bertha.

Gray skies hung above Seattle on Groundhog Day 2019 as the city prepared to celebrate the opening of Bertha's tunnel. Early that morning, the groundhog had left his burrow without seeing his shadow, predicting an early spring.

Bertha had also left her place underground, predicting a new era of safety in Seattle. Instead of driving on a rickety highway, Seattleites would travel through a tunnel specially designed to withstand an earthquake. Greg likes to point out, "If there's ever an earthquake, the tunnel is the safest place to be."

The day was full of warm reunions for Greg and the other crew members. They watched the governor cut the ribbon in front of the tunnel, and then they marched inside for a firsthand look at what they had helped Bertha build.

Greg had always seen the tunnel as a work of art,
and it turned out as beautifully as he had imagined.

However, you can't always trust a groundhog. The very next afternoon, a wet snow blanketed Seattle, coating the trees and slicking over the streets. But the Seattleites didn't need to worry about an earthquake or the snow.

Just after midnight, Bertha's tunnel opened to traffic for the first time. Happy travelers in their cars zoomed through the tunnel, grateful to find a safe and dry path under the city. All thanks to Bertha.

In April 2017, workers pose with Bertha at the end of their long journey together.

DIGGING THE TUNNEL

Big Bertha follows the story of civil engineer Greg Hauser's involvement with Bertha and the completion of the SR 99 tunnel that replaced the Alaskan Way Viaduct. However, this enormous project was the result of hundreds of people working and coordinating together. Different types of engineers in Japan and the United States, electricians, laborers that performed a variety of trades, teamsters that drove trucks and buses, administrators, inspectors, and many unseen people joined together to gift this beautiful tunnel to the people of Seattle.

BERTHA'S UNBELIEVABLE NUMBERS

LENGTH: 326 feet, about the size of a large Washington State Ferry or a football field

HEIGHT: 57.5 feet, the height of a 5-story building

WEIGHT: 6,700 tons, the weight of 35 blue whales

WIDTH OF LARGEST BOULDER THAT BERTHA COULD SWALLOW: 3 feet

AMOUNT OF SOIL DUG OUT OF THE TUNNEL BY BERTHA: 850,000 cubic yards; if this soil were piled into Lumen Field, it would make a mountain of dirt 100 feet taller than the stadium's roof!

PEOPLE WORKING WITH BERTHA EVERY SHIFT: 25

EARTHQUAKE MAGNITUDE THAT BERTHA'S TUNNEL WAS DESIGNED TO SURVIVE: 9.0

2001 EARTHQUAKE MAGNITUDE THAT DAMAGED THE VIADUCT: 6.8

LENGTH OF TUNNEL BERTHA DUG: 1.7 miles

HOW FAR BERTHA COULD DIG IN A DAY: 35 feet

IF YOU EVER DRIVE THROUGH BERTHA'S TUNNEL ...

Be sure to look up at the ceiling.

If you are driving southbound, you will see a curved ceiling above you, which is the arching walls of the outside of the tunnel. You are driving on the upper deck of the roadway.

If you are traveling northbound, you will see a flat ceiling overhead, which is the underside of the southbound roadway above you. You are driving on the lower deck of the roadway.

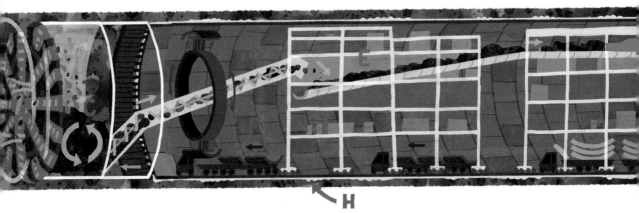

H

HOW BERTHA DUG AND BUILT A TUNNEL AT THE SAME TIME

Bertha was an earth pressure balance tunnel boring machine often referred to as a TBM (tunnel boring machine). Sometimes tunnels are dug first and then the tunnel walls are added later. Having a machine like Bertha that could dig and build the tunnel at the same time made the process much faster and more efficient. Bertha completed her mission by following the steps below.

A Bertha's cutterhead rotated, causing her teeth to grind and break up the soil ahead of her.

B Foamy conditioners sprayed out of her cutterhead, mixing with the loosened soil to create muck, which was much thicker and easier to move than loose soil alone.

C The muck was sucked into the mixing chamber behind Bertha's cutterhead where it was mixed with more conditioners.

D The soil transportation screw pulled the muck out of the mixing chamber and dumped it onto a belt conveyor.

E The belt conveyor carried the muck out Bertha's back end and eventually out of the tunnel where it was loaded onto barges and carried away. As Bertha's tunnel grew longer and longer, the belt conveyor had to be extended as well.

F At Bertha's back end, rubber-tired vehicles carried in the concrete segments Bertha needed to build the outside walls of the tunnel. Her two erector arms placed these arcs of concrete together, creating two-foot-thick concrete rings, one ring at a time. To increase the strength of the tunnel, the seams of the concrete arcs were staggered with the seams from the previous ring, like bricks on a wall.

G Once a ring was complete, Bertha used her hydraulic rams to push off, driving herself forward and exposing the ring that had been inside her outer shield.

H The space that remained between the outside of the ring and the earth was then pressure-filled with fast-hardening grout to waterproof and strengthen the tunnel wall.

BERTHA'S TWO-THOUSAND-YEAR-OLD TECHNOLOGY

Why is Bertha's tunnel so strong? The rings of her tunnel are similar to the stone arches built more than two thousand years ago by the Romans, many of which are so sturdy they still stand today. An arched bridge is stronger than a flat bridge because, in a flat bridge, all the weight of the bridge pushes straight downward.

In an arched bridge, some of the downward weight is transferred outward to the sides due to the shape of the stones. Buttresses on the outside of an arched bridge then push back and keep the bridge from collapsing.

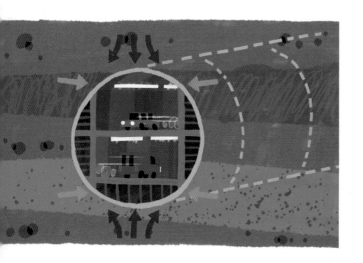

In Bertha's tunnel, any inward force is partially transferred to the sides just as in an arch. The strong earth surrounding the tunnel acts like a buttress, pushing back and keeping the tunnel from collapsing inward.

BERTHA'S SOUNDS

As a safety measure, Bertha was designed so that anytime she was about to start moving, she would play music to alert the workers in the area. Songs on Bertha's playlist included: "Mary Had a Little Lamb," "We've Only Just Begun" by the Carpenters, and music by Beethoven.

BERTHA'S BREAKDOWN CAUSED A FUSS

There has been much debate about what caused Bertha to break down. Was it a pipe buried in the ground that she hit? Was there a problem with her design? Was her machinery operated incorrectly? Was the uneven soil under Seattle too much for even our most current and advanced technology? All these questions and the enormous cost of this big tunnel project caused much conflict between the city of Seattle and the companies that built and operated Bertha. At the end of a long legal battle about who would pay the extra costs resulting from Bertha's delays and repairs, the courts ruled in favor of the city of Seattle. The decision stated that the company that dug the tunnel would have to pay on account of mistakes that were made.

DIGGING DEEPER

Check out these resources to find out more about Bertha and tunnels.

Book
Bridges and Tunnels: Investigate Feats of Engineering with 25 Projects by Donna Latham. White River Junction, VT: Nomad Press, 2012.

Search on YouTube
"SR 99 'Smart' Tunnel"

"Alaskan Way Viaduct—Tunnel Boring Animation"

"Bye-Bye to Bertha, the world's largest tunneling machine"

For my sistah, who always digs
in and keeps going. —A.A.

For Michael, the little
lion man. —K.W.

Copyright © 2024 by Amanda Abler
Illustrations copyright © 2024 by Katy Wu

All rights reserved. No portion of this book may be
reproduced or utilized in any form, or by any electronic,
mechanical, or other means, without the prior written
permission of the publisher.

Printed in China by Dream Colour Printing Ltd.
in April 2024

LITTLE BIGFOOT with colophon is a registered trademark
of Penguin Random House LLC

28 27 26 25 24   9 8 7 6 5 4 3 2 1

Editors: Ben Clanton and Christy Cox
Production editor: Isabella Hardie
Designer: Anna Goldstein
Photo of Bertha and her crew © WSDOT

Library of Congress Cataloging-in-Publication
Data is available.

ISBN: 978-1-63217-306-5

Sasquatch Books
1325 Fourth Avenue, Suite 1025
Seattle, WA 98101

SasquatchBooks.com

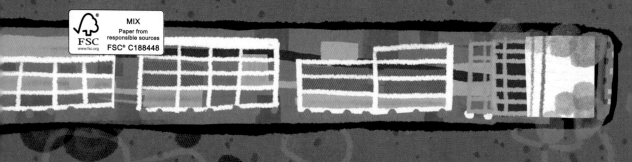